SPACE STATIONS
and Other Exploration Tech

Co-published by agreement between Shi Tu Hui and World Book, Inc.

Shi Tu Hui
Room 1807, Block 1,
#3 West Dawang Road
Chaoyang District, Beijing 100025
P.R. China

World Book, Inc.
180 North LaSalle Street
Suite 900
Chicago, Illinois 60601
USA

Copyright © 2024. All rights reserved. This volume may not be reproduced in whole or in part in any form without prior written permission from the publishers.

WORLD BOOK and the GLOBE DEVICE are registered trademarks or trademarks of World Book, Inc.

Library of Congress Cataloging-in-Publication Data for this volume has been applied for.

Cool Tech (set, hardcover)
ISBN: 978-0-7166-5479-7

Space Stations and Other Exploration Tech
ISBN: 978-0-7166-5485-8 (hardcover)
ISBN: 978-0-7166-5497-1 (softcover)
ISBN: 978-0-7166-5491-9 (e-book)

Written by Richard Spilsbury

STAFF

VP, Editorial: Tom Evans

Manager, New Product: Nicholas Kilzer

Curriculum Designer: Caroline Davidson

Proofreader: Nathalie Strassheim

Coordinator, Design Development & Production: Brenda Tropinski

Digital Asset Specialist: Rosalia Bledsoe

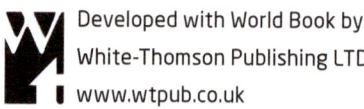
Developed with World Book by
White-Thomson Publishing LTD
www.wtpub.co.uk

ACKNOWLEDGMENTS

Cover	© Science Photo Library/Alamy Images
5	© 3Dsculptor/Shutterstock
6-7	© Vast Space; NASA
8-9	NASA; Indian Space Research Organization; © Axiom Space; © Alejo Miranda, Shutterstock
10-11	© Airbus; © Northrop Grumman; © Sierra Space
12-13	© Starlab; © Voyager Space Holdings; NASA
14-15	NASA; Canadian Space Agency
16-17	© ClearSpace SA; NASA Orbital Debris Program Office; NASA; © Nanoracks
18-19	© Gorodenkoff/Shutterstock; © Polaris Program
20-21	NASA; © Blue Origin
22-23	NASA; Corey Green, U.S. Navy; © Paopano/Shutterstock
24-25	© Axiom Space; SpaceX; © Blue Origin; NASA/Jet Propulsion Laboratory, California Institute of Technology
26-27	© Skorzewiak/Shutterstock; Ministry of Science and ICT
28-29	ESA/ATG; NASA/Johns Hopkins University/Carnegie Institution of Washington; CU/LASP EMM/EXI ITF/Kevin M. Gill; ESA/ATG; NASA/ESA/J. Nichols (University of Leicester); NASA/JPL; NASA/JPL/University of Arizona
30-33	NASA
34-35	© Intuitive Machines; © Embry-Riddle Aeronautical University
36-37	© ispace Inc.; NASA
38-39	NASA
40-41	CNSA
42-43	© GMTO Corporation; © Firefly Aerospace
44-45	NASA; ESA; © Alexander Madurowicz, Stanford University

CONTENTS

Acknowledgments 2

Glossary 4

Introduction 5

1. Space Stations 6
2. Space Exploration 18
3. Probes 26
4. Robot Landers and Rovers 34
5. Space Observatories 42

Resources 46

Index 48

> There is a glossary of terms on the first page. Terms defined in the glossary are in boldface type **that looks like this** on their first appearance in the book.

GLOSSARY

airlock a chamber with two airtight openings to permit passage between two spaces of unequal atmospheric pressure.

autonomous designed to operate independently without control by others or by outside forces.

biomanufacturing the use of biological systems and organisms engineered or otherwise used to produce a product.

corona the outermost layer of the sun's atmosphere.

CubeSat a miniaturized satellite constructed of modular cube-shaped components.

ionize in chemistry and physics, any process by which electrically neutral atoms or molecules are converted to electrically charged atoms or molecules (ions) through gaining or losing electrons.

low Earth orbit (LEO) an orbital path around Earth with an altitude that lies toward the lower end of the range of possible orbits. This is typically around 1,200 miles (2,000 kilometers) or less.

modular constructed in similar sizes or with similar units for flexibility and variety in use.

module a self-contained unit of a spacecraft.

orbit a regular, repeating path that one object in space takes around another one. An object in an orbit is called a satellite or an orbiter.

orbiter a spacecraft designed to go into orbit, especially one not intended to land.

payload the scientific or technological instruments carried on board a satellite.

radiation energy given off in the form of waves or tiny particles of matter. Radiation is found throughout the universe. It comes in many forms.

regolith a layer of loose, unconsolidated rock and dust that sits on top of a layer of solid rock.

retro thruster a small rocket engine on a larger rocket or spacecraft that produces thrust in the opposite direction to the direction of flight, in order to decelerate the vehicle or make it move backward.

satellite a human-made object launched by rocket into an orbit around Earth or another body.

solar cell a device that converts solar radiation into electricity.

INTRODUCTION

Imagine a future where space exploration is an everyday event, when we better understand the mysteries of the sun, our solar system, and distant galaxies. Imagine scheduled trips from Earth to ferry visitors to busy science hubs and hotels in space, a future when colonization of the moon and even scheduled trips to Mars are a reality.

Space is often called the final frontier. Maybe. But today, space is certainly a new frontier that many countries and private companies are trying to explore. Space promises new territories to occupy and resources to harvest—and scientific discoveries that add to our knowledge of Earth's place in the universe.

Space stations are the biggest orbiting structures we have ever built. For now, these are the hubs for human activity in space. They hold the science labs and places for people to test the effects of space conditions on life. Yet space stations are just a small part of our space exploration technologies. New space tech ranges from baseball-sized rover vehicles to deep space craft. This book looks at the ways space technology is shaping our understanding of our universe now and into the future.

1 SPACE STATIONS

HOME AWAY FROM HOME

Space stations are the first human outposts in space. They offer the immersive experience of living in microgravity (weightlessness) high above Earth. A space station is bigger than a spacecraft and remains in **orbit** without returning to Earth. Space stations do not travel far beyond Earth's orbit or land on other objects. As of 2023, there are two fully operational space stations orbiting Earth—the International Space Station (ISS), launched in 1998, and China's new Tiangong Space Station (TSS). Several others are planned for the near future.

Space stations are usually built out of **modules** transported into orbit on rockets. Astronauts typically spend weeks or months on a space station. For this reason, space stations must offer comfortable living conditions. Supplies are regularly sent to a space station by cargo craft launched from Earth.

Life on a space station relies on Environmental Control and Life Support Systems (ECLSS) to artificially control the atmosphere. Collins Aerospace's next-generation ECLSS fits into special racks about half the size of those currently in use on the ISS. Their new Air Revitalization System rack removes carbon dioxide (CO_2) and other air contaminants, and controls temperature and humidity. Other racks generate oxygen and recycle water from urine. This reduces the amount of oxygen and water that must be transported to the station. Rack components are easy to access and can easily be controlled wirelessly.

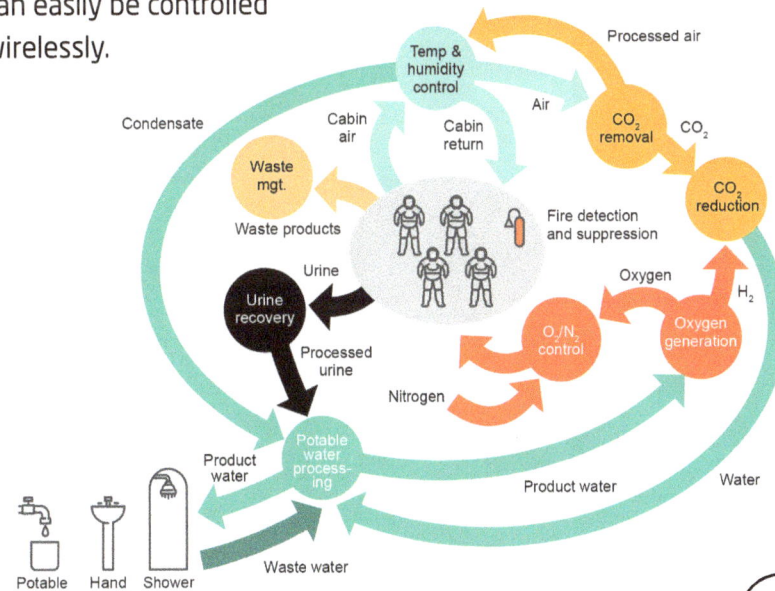

INTERNATIONAL AND NATIONAL SPACE STATIONS

For 25 years, the ISS has been the greatest showcase of space technology. It is the largest peacetime engineering project, constructed from modules by many nations. More than 260 astronauts have lived on board ISS over many missions. But the reign of the ISS is coming to an end. New high-tech space stations are poised to take over.

The last day is approaching for the ISS. The decades of intense temperature changes and space **radiation** are taking their toll, as are the stresses caused by docking and undocking spacecraft. ISS is also gradually falling out of orbit. It is not a powered spacecraft, and the drag of Earth's gravity is overcoming its orbiting speed. Visiting spacecraft occasionally give it a boost to stay in orbit, but that adds even more stress. So ISS controllers plan to maneuver the space station out of orbit in 2030. By 2031, it will enter Earth's atmosphere. Some pieces will burn up, but the rest will fall into the ocean far from populated areas.

Next-generation station. Parts are still being added to the ISS. One of the modules due to join the ISS is an Axiom habitat module. This is designed as living quarters for visiting astronauts. But mission planners expect that, one day, it will be part of a new space station! Before the space station ends its mission, Axiom will disconnect from ISS and connect to other Axiom modules to form a new station. The new free-flying station will generate its own power using **solar cells**.

New kid on the block. The Chinese Space Station (CSS) was launched into Earth orbit in 2021. The CSS has several state-of-the-art technologies that set it apart from the ISS. About one-fifth the size of the ISS, the CSS can house three taikonauts (the Chinese term for space explorers). The CSS has two steerable solar power arrays (banks of solar cells that twist toward the sun) on each module. The angle chosen maximizes power generation while reducing heat buildup that can damage sensitive equipment. On the ISS, the solar arrays are fixed and need radiators to dissipate built-up heat.

Space presence. Other countries are also planning space stations. India has already launched and returned a crewed spacecraft. India plans to have its own operational space station by 2030. Russia has a long history operating space stations. Russia collaborated on the ISS, but the nation now wants to go it alone. The new Russian Orbital Space Station is planned for launch by 2025.

COMMERCIAL SPACE STATIONS

There is such vast commercial potential in space exploration that a generation of bold new companies is planning private space station missions. Some are sending up swarms of communications and global positioning system (GPS) **satellites** into orbit to create a station made of many parts. Others are designing space stations to rival those produced by the United States, Russia, and China that will be ready for launch in the next decade.

LOOP. The European multinational company Airbus is designing a space station that will be constructed as an all-in-one circular unit called LOOP. The LOOP station is 26 feet (8 meters) wide, and it fits onto a SpaceX Super Heavy rocket so it can be launched as a single piece. This is much less expensive than constructing a station from individual modules. LOOP has three decks joined by a connecting tunnel. The tunnel overlooks a space glasshouse that will be used for plant-growing experiments in space. The station includes a habitation deck, a science deck, and a centrifuge deck. The centrifuge deck spins on an axis to create artificial gravity to provide astronauts relief from the effects of microgravity (weightlessness) on long missions.

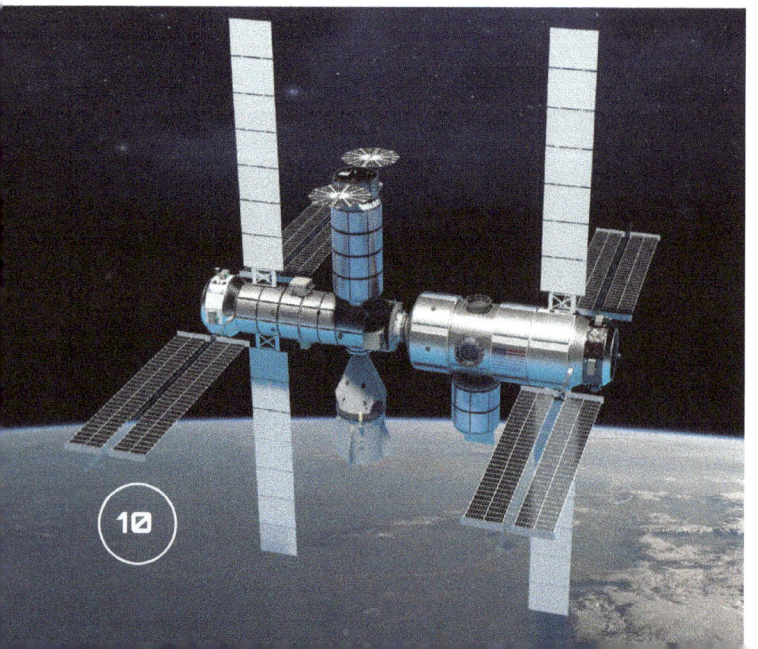

Complete service. The Northrop Grumman space station plans to offer a complete service for companies who want an inroad into space. The station itself can host eight people and has six docking ports for visiting spacecraft. Northrop Grumman also offers add-on services like crew training, cargo drops, and payload recovery. Extensive onboard science research facilities are developed in collaboration with a biotechnology research company, Rhodium Scientific. The company plans to offer facilities for **biomanufacturing** in space.

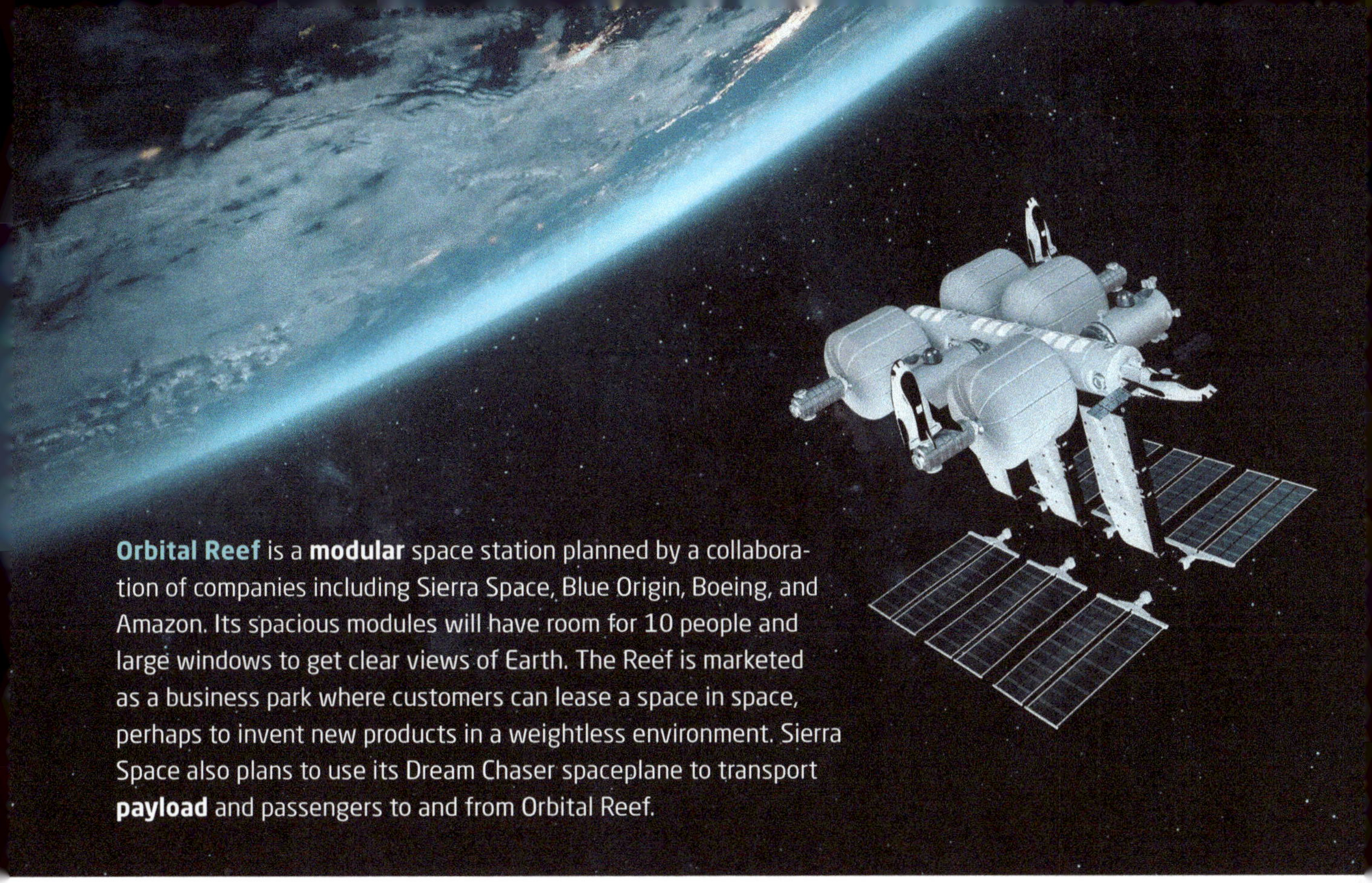

Orbital Reef is a **modular** space station planned by a collaboration of companies including Sierra Space, Blue Origin, Boeing, and Amazon. Its spacious modules will have room for 10 people and large windows to get clear views of Earth. The Reef is marketed as a business park where customers can lease a space in space, perhaps to invent new products in a weightless environment. Sierra Space also plans to use its Dream Chaser spaceplane to transport **payload** and passengers to and from Orbital Reef.

LIFE. Large Integrated Flexible Environment (LIFE) habitat modules are innovative protective bubbles where people can live on Orbital Reef. These will be launched into orbit as small units around 15 feet (5 meters) wide. LIFE modules are locked onto the central part of Orbital Reef and inflated into doughnut-shaped modules. LIFE modules are made from an inner airtight layer and a reinforcing middle layer of flexible woven fabric called Vectran that is stronger than steel. Outer layers protect against temperature extremes and impact from space debris. Onboard control systems circulate air, control temperature, and provide lighting.

STARLAB

Anyone can rent a space on one of the planned commercial space stations. But Starlab is a little different. It will be the first continuously crewed commercial space station available for hire. Starlab is being developed by Nanoracks, Voyager Space, and Lockheed Martin. It will serve the needs of the United States National Aeronautics and Space Administration (NASA) and other space agencies worldwide. This game-changing station is due for launch into orbit in 2028.

Science park. The Starlab space station will include a large inflatable crew habitat that can accommodate four astronauts, a docking port, a power and propulsion element, and a large robotic arm for moving cargo and payloads. Starlab is also the future home of the George Washington Carver (GWC) Science Park, a state-of-the-art science laboratory.

Earth analog. Scientists on Starlab will conduct research and experiments in biology, plant science, and materials research with a wide variety of applications. The research will be coordinated with an analog laboratory on Earth at the Ohio State University. The analog laboratory will be a replica of the Starlab space station science park, and it will allow researchers to conduct parallel experiments on the ground. Scientists can design experiments and models on Earth and test them in space.

Luxury stay. Gone are the days when astronauts lived in uncomfortable, cramped conditions. One of Starlab's partners is Hilton, the global hotel group. Hilton plans to design luxury habitation including sleeping quarters, hospitality suites, and communal areas for resident astronauts and visitors. But Hilton also has an eye on the future of hospitality. Hilton will use its experience on Starlab to research and design the technology to build a hotel in space.

Private/public partnerships are common in space programs due to the high costs involved. Governments collaborate with companies to develop space programs to spread the costs and share expertise. For example, NASA used Northrop Grumman's aircraft design expertise to make spaceplanes. Nanoracks initially produced a range of payloads for the ISS, including devices to launch small satellites. In 2020, its Bishop **airlock** became the first permanent commercial add-on equipment on the ISS. The airlock is a circular unit to host small space labs or deploy satellites into space. Now Nanoracks is bringing its expertise to NASA for use on Starlab.

LUNAR GATEWAY

Most space stations orbit hundreds of miles above Earth in **low Earth orbit (LEO).** But Lunar Gateway is planned to orbit the moon far from the pull of Earth's gravity. It will be the first *extraterrestrial* (beyond Earth) space station.

The Artemis program is a mission to return humans to the moon and beyond. The first aim is to establish a human presence on and near the moon, to study the moon in greater detail, to reap its economic benefits, and to inspire a new generation of explorers. But another aim is to use that experience as a springboard for crewed missions to our nearest planet, Mars! Artemis technology includes spacecraft to get to Mars and land there, a planned base camp named Outpost built on the moon, and Gateway.

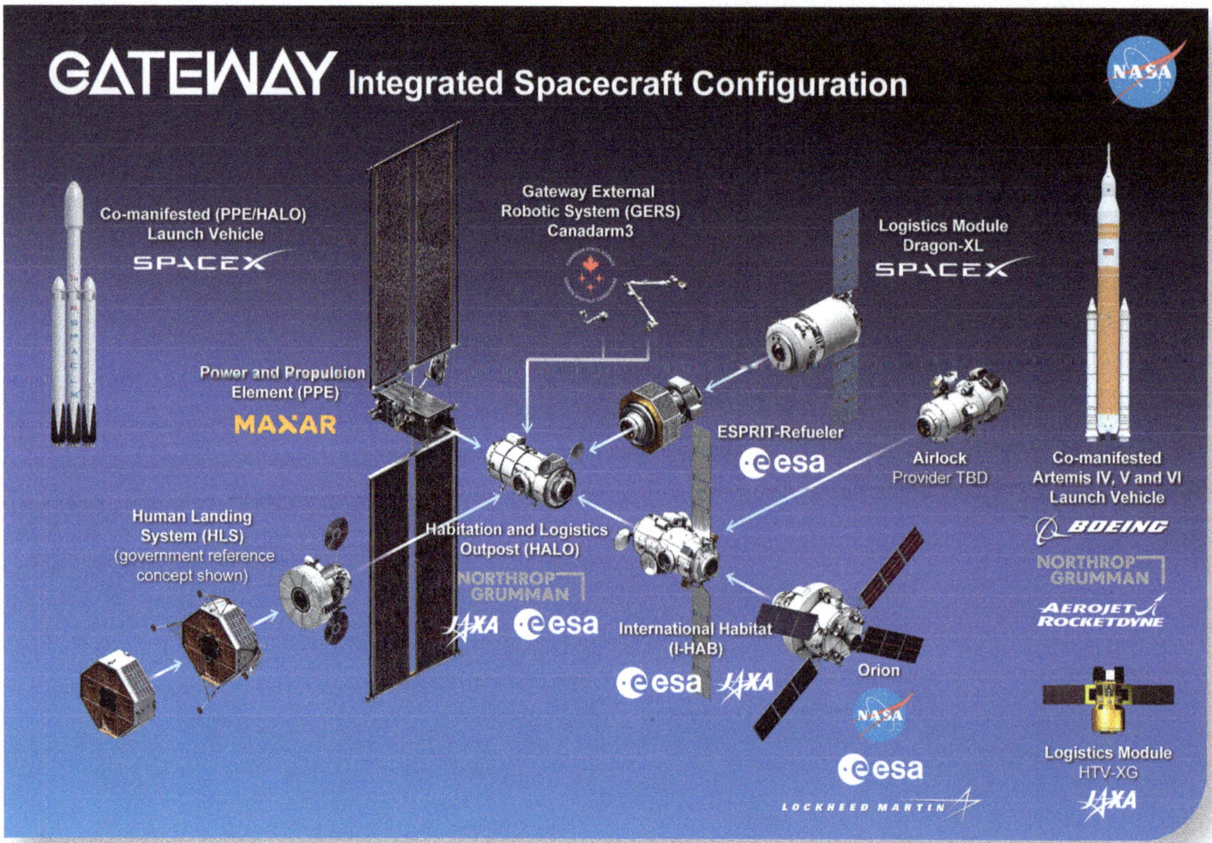

Moving station. Gateway will stay in orbit and at the correct altitude and move above the moon using its power and propulsion element (PPE). This uses solar electric propulsion. Solar power from solar arrays powers the PPE's thrusters to **ionize** xenon gas. This creates an exhaust plume of xenon ions moving at over 65,000 miles per hour (18,000 kilometers per hour) to move the space station. The solar electric thrusters will deliver three times more power for a given mass of fuel than current thruster designs. The PPE also uses solar power to generate electricity to operate instruments and provide a communications relay for human and robotic expeditions to the lunar surface.

Say HALO. The astronauts on Gateway will rely on HALO—the Habitation and Logistics Outpost module where they will live and conduct their experiments. HALO safety features include life support systems that ensure that the atmosphere, pressure, temperature, and water supply are carefully managed. HALO includes a fire suppression system and is also the command center of the station. It has control systems for Outpost and docking ports for supply spacecraft and lunar landers.

Smart arms. Gateway will use the Canada-supplied Canadarm3 robotic arm to handle payload. Its design builds on the success of the previous generation Canadarms on the ISS. Canadarm3 is made up of smaller and larger arms. The smaller arm transfers mission-critical payload from outside to inside Gateway through a port. The larger arm will help visiting spacecraft dock. Computers in the arms use artificial intelligence to coordinate tasks. Parts of the smaller arm can even be swapped to help maintain the larger arm. In return for Canada's contribution, one of the first Artemis mission astronauts landing on the moon will be Canadian!

SPACE JUNK

Space stations and satellites are not the only objects in LEO. There is also an orbiting junkyard made up of debris, old satellites, and rocket stages. The junkyard will grow as commercial space missions become more common. That's why exciting new technologies are emerging to dispose of the junk.

Cleanup. ClearSpace-1 is a mission to build, launch, and fly a space junk chaser by 2025! The chaser is an **autonomous** (self-controlled) spacecraft fitted with four robotic arms. It will grab abandoned or damaged satellites and deorbit them. This means it will carry the load down into the atmosphere where both craft will burn up and fall harmlessly to Earth. The mission was commissioned by the European Space Agency (ESA). In the past, astronauts used robotic arms on the space shuttle to remove debris from orbit. But this is an expensive, time-consuming, and risky task for astronauts. If the initial mission proves successful, future ClearSpace craft may be able to dispose of space junk without disposing of themselves!

Ever-present threat. Orbiting space junk is a threat to space stations and the people living and working there. Objects orbiting Earth travel faster than a bullet fired from a gun. The force of impact from even a tiny space object can be immense. In 2021, a Chinese weather satellite was destroyed by the impact of a 4-inch (10-centimeter) piece of debris from a Russian rocket that had been orbiting for 25 years! In 2022, NASA reported that the ISS has executed 32 course corrections just to avoid space junk. NASA aims to develop a "space tug" to maneuver the ISS safely out of orbit at its end of life. This will prevent ISS from becoming space junk itself.

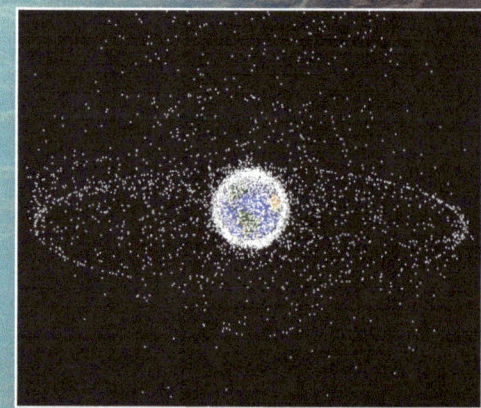

Trash space station. Another space junk solution is to use it to build a space station! Nanorack's Outpost space stations will be built into the discarded upper stages of rockets. Nanoracks' Mission Extension Kit (MEK) is fitted into the rocket stage before launch. It is activated once the stage exhausts its fuel and is discarded. Under MEK control, the stage can be turned into a scientific or residential module. In 2022, Nanoracks and Voyager Space demonstrated metal cutting in space for the first time, using a circular saw on a robotic arm. This technology will be key to cutting into the fuel tank and creating custom Outpost modules.

Reuse and repair is as important in space as it is on Earth for saving resources and reducing pollution. Zombie satellites are satellites with functional systems that have run out of fuel and are orbiting as junk. A new Mission Extension Vehicle (MEV) from Northrop Grumman can dock onto a nonfunctioning satellite. Then it moves the satellite into the correct orbit, so the satellite can be reused. The OSAM-1 spacecraft goes one step further. It will grasp, refuel, and relocate satellites to extend their lives. A robotic arm named SPIDER will be able to repair broken parts and construct new ones, such as communications antennae.

2 SPACE EXPLORATION

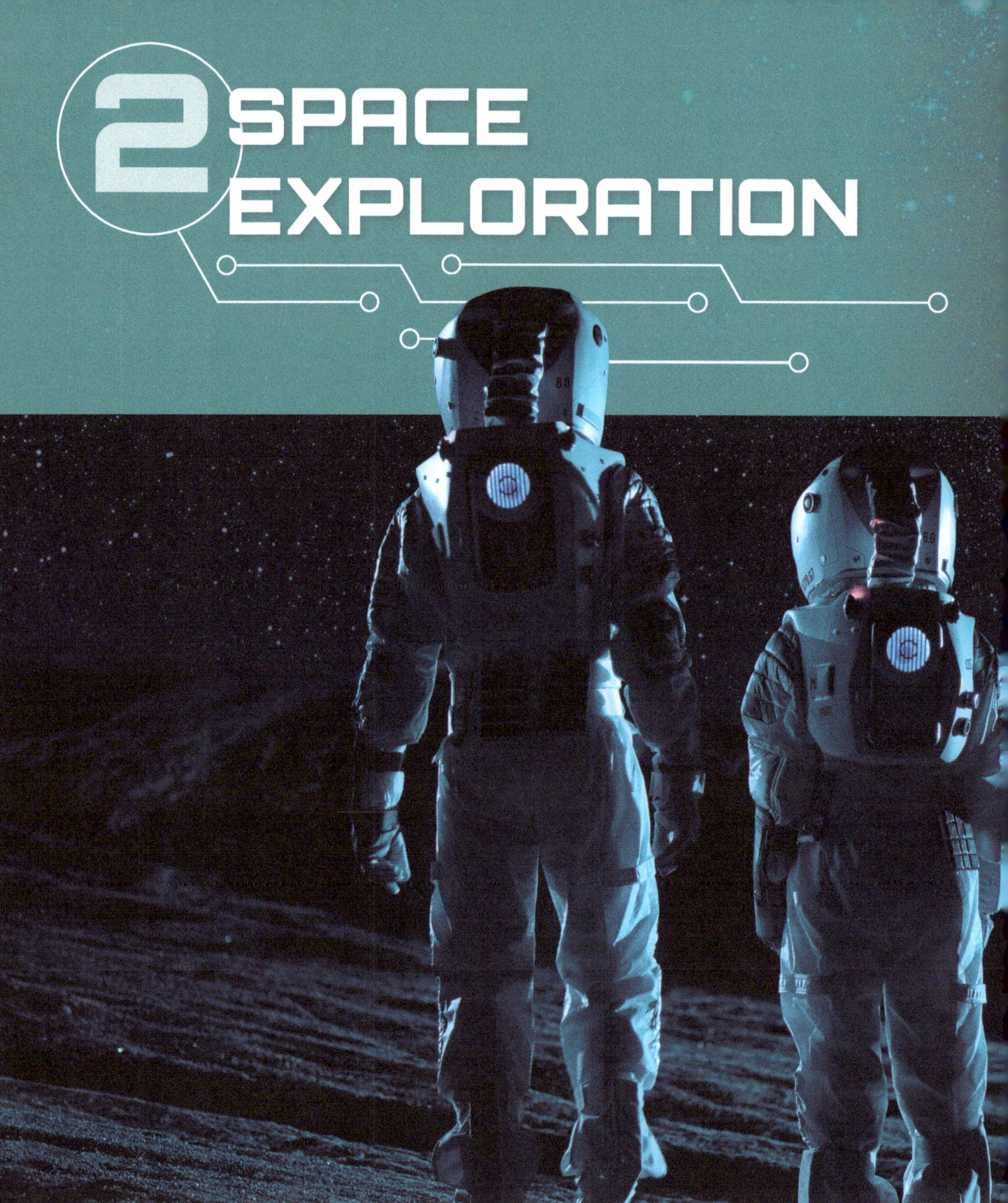

PREPARING TO GO FARTHER

It's been a while, but we are going back to deep space! There has been no manned space exploration beyond LEO since 1972 when the last astronauts landed on the moon. Several companies are planning new space exploration missions. They are developing the necessary technology and spacecraft to transport humans into and back from space. This technology includes orbiting space stations and habitation modules. Many nations and companies plan to go beyond Earth's moon to explore Mars.

Companies are investigating resources on the moon to use for building habitation and infrastructure needed to use the moon as a space base for longer interplanetary voyages. Other companies are developing and testing the technology needed to send humans on long, deep space missions to Mars.

In 2023, a commercial mission named Polaris Dawn will reach the highest Earth orbit yet. The spaceship will orbit around 435 miles (700 kilometers) above Earth. Four people will emerge through the airlock for the world's first private spacewalk. In space, the crew will conduct medical experiments to help plan future human space flights. For example, they will use an ultrasound machine to scan the eye to detect whether low gravity affects vision.

TRANSPORTATION TECHNOLOGY

Launching astronauts into space requires a capable transportation spacecraft that rides on a powerful rocket. These remarkable vehicles combine safety for the crew with good maneuverability and power. And they must also be capable of returning the astronauts to Earth!

Enter the Dragon. The SpaceX Dragon spacecraft has proven its abilities on more than 35 trips to the ISS. This smooth craft can carry up to seven passengers to and from Earth orbit and beyond. Dragon is a small powerhouse. It has 16 Draco thrusters to maneuver the craft, with extra power for emergencies. The SpaceX Dragon can return to Earth with up to 6,614 pounds (3,000 kilograms) of cargo. Tough blast shields on the outside protect Dragon and its occupants from the intense heat of reentry. Upon return, high above Earth, two sets of parachutes deploy. These slow the craft as it splashes down into the ocean.

Next-gen crew craft. In 2020, a prototype next-generation spacecraft was launched into orbit. This spacecraft was built to carry taikonauts to the Chinese space station and even the moon. The prototype flew as expected and returned to Earth. At reentry, the capsule was oriented so it skipped along the edge of Earth's atmosphere a little like a stone thrown across a pond. This pushed the craft back into space where it cooled. Then it was ready to reenter and descend to Earth.

Pilot-free. New Shepard is a reusable spacecraft designed to carry space tourists to the boundary of space on the trip of a lifetime. The passenger capsule at the top has large windows so tourists can see their journey to the edge of space. New Shepard is fully autonomous. Its maneuvers are fully programmed, and the occupants have no control over the craft. The capsule detaches once it reaches the edge of space, and the launch rocket returns to Earth. The rocket has **retro thrusters** and air brakes to slow its descent as it lands vertically on the ground on fold-out landing gear. The passenger capsule descends and lands in the ocean with the aid of parachutes.

Deep space missions require efficient engines that provide more thrust for higher speed to shorten space journeys, so that crews spend less time exposed to space radiation. Nuclear thermal propulsion (NTP) engines use a nuclear reactor to superheat liquid hydrogen into gas. The gas expands from a nozzle to provide propulsion. NTP propulsion is twice as powerful as current spacecraft engines. Scientists estimate that improved NTP's could cut down on travel time for crewed missions to Mars from 9 months using current technology to 45 days!

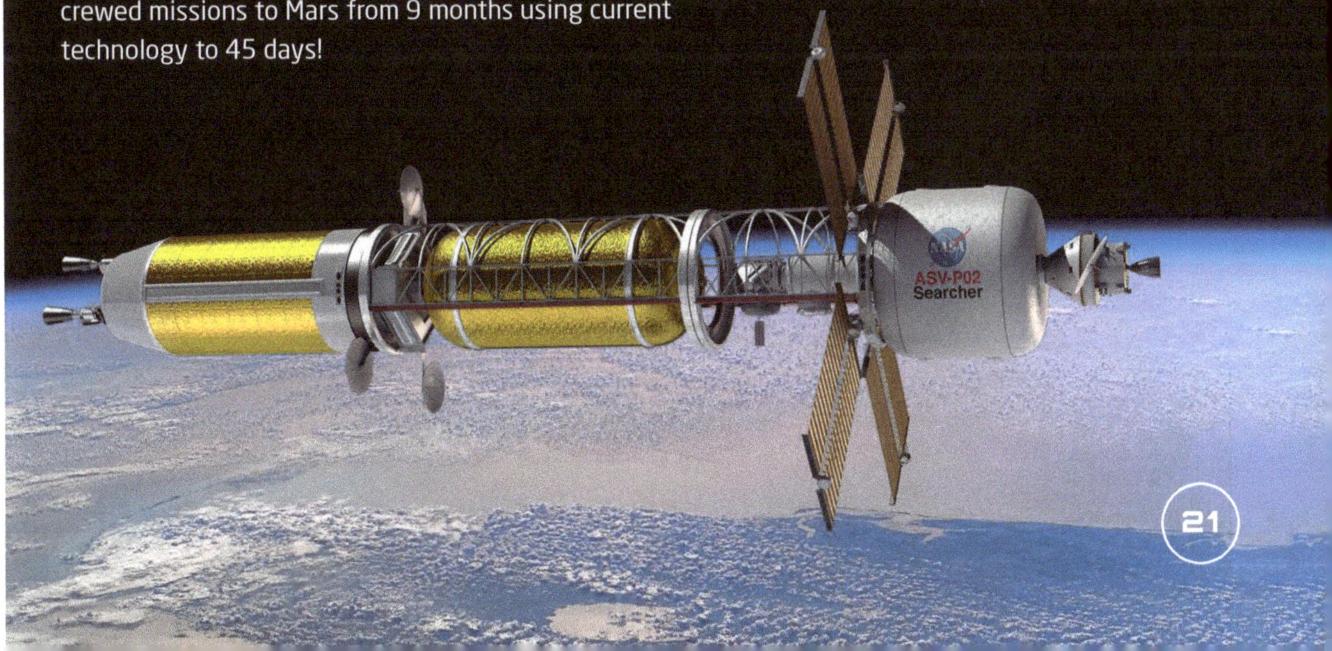

ORION

Today, Orion is the only spacecraft capable of a deep space mission to the moon and a high-speed return to Earth. Orion is a versatile, reusable spacecraft designed to last several decades. On the first Artemis mission in 2022, Orion traveled thousands of miles beyond the moon autonomously. Orion will take astronauts on a moon flyby in 2024. And in 2028, Orion will enable the first moon landing since the 1970's. Orion is bristling with new technology to ensure successful mission completion.

Crew module. Orion's three modules include a center crew module. Four crew will live and work in this sealed, airtight module on their journey to the moon and back. The capsule provides a safe habitat for a planned three-week mission and return to Earth. Lockers containing food, medical kits, emergency equipment such as fire extinguishers, and sleeping bags are kept under the seats. Astronauts will wear space suits designed to reduce the high-pressure effects created during launch and return. A titanium blast shield coated with AVCOAT sits underneath the crew module. This heatproof coating burns off during reentry to help cool the module.

Launch Abort System. Orion is propelled into space on the enormous Space Launch System (SLS) rocket—more powerful than any previous rocket. The pointed device on top of the crew module is its safety net. During launch, it protects the capsule and disconnects once Orion is in space. In the event of a launch abort warning—when the whole rocket could explode—something else happens. Three thrusters automatically fire. They accelerate the crew module from 0 to 500 miles per hour (800 kilometers per hour) within 2 seconds to safety away from the rocket body. That's three times faster than the speed of the catapult firing a fighter jet from an aircraft carrier.

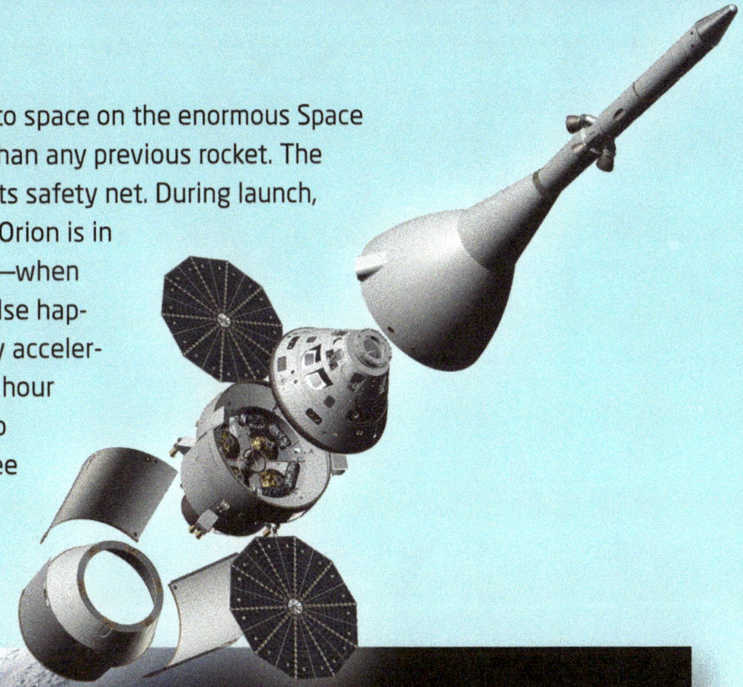

Powerhouse. Another Orion module is the cylindrical service module. This module has a main thruster for propulsion on its base. Thirty smaller thrusters control Orion's speed, trajectory (path), and orientation—all controlled by a central computer. Four solar arrays around the module's edge generate electricity for the life support systems.

Avionics are the basic electronic systems that make flight possible and safe. Orion's avionics incorporate vehicle management computers to control the spacecraft. The avionics also execute commands sent from Earth or by the crew. The avionics include a guidance, navigation, and control system to control the craft's position, destination, and orientation. The system navigates via GPS when close to Earth. In deep space, Orion locks onto NASA's Deep Space Network—a network of giant tracking antennae around the world that determine Orion's location.

LUNAR LIFE

Humans have always dreamed of living on the moon. Spacecraft like Orion are only part of the technology needed for a program to colonize the moon. New high-tech landing craft, astronaut suits, and living quarters will be vital for lunar life.

Landing craft. NASA has selected several designs of lunar landers or human landing systems (HLS) for the Artemis mission. SpaceX's HLS is a Starship adapted for a vertical moon landing. It carries astronauts from Earth to the moon and back in a spacious cabin near the top. Two airlocks allow astronauts to leave or enter the ship. The Dynetics/Northrop Grumman HLS is another horizontal spacecraft designed to operate near the moon and dock with Orion for astronaut transfer.

Space suits. Axiom Space's Extravehicular Mobility Unit, or AxEMU, is a new kind of fabric space suit to protect astronauts from heat, radiation, and particles. The suit provides air and optimal pressure without the bulk and rigidity of traditional space suits. AxEMU has innovative joints for greater flexibility and mobility. The large, clear helmet provides a wide-screen view with built-in lighting and a high-definition camera. The actual AxEMU will be white to reflect heat.

Dust is a big problem on the moon. Moon dust, or **regolith,** is made as the hard surface rock is struck by tiny meteoroids over thousands of years. The regolith is electrostatically charged by space radiation. This means that it sticks easily to landers, space suits, and other technology. Moon dust is difficult to brush off and easily clogs seals and moving parts. The dust's jagged edges can wear away suit fabric and surfaces. To combat this problem, NASA has developed a moon duster—a handheld device that fires an electron beam. The beam creates a charge that repels the dust from surfaces.

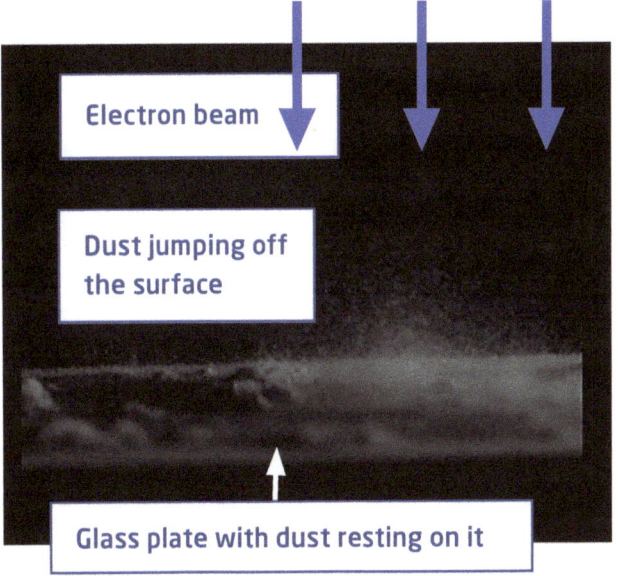

Living off the land. Regolith is also a valuable resource. By mass, it is almost half oxygen trapped in various minerals. The Blue Alchemist program from Blue Origin plans to make power-generating solar cells from regolith using molten regolith electrolysis (MRE). In MRE, regolith is melted at high temperatures with an electrical current sent through the liquid. This causes a chemical reaction that splits the regolith into oxygen gas and other materials, such as silicon. Blue Alchemist has demonstrated that this process can produce pure silicon used for making solar cells and glass to protect the panels. Using resources and materials from the moon is much less expensive compared to making materials on Earth and transporting them to the moon on spacecraft.

3 PROBES

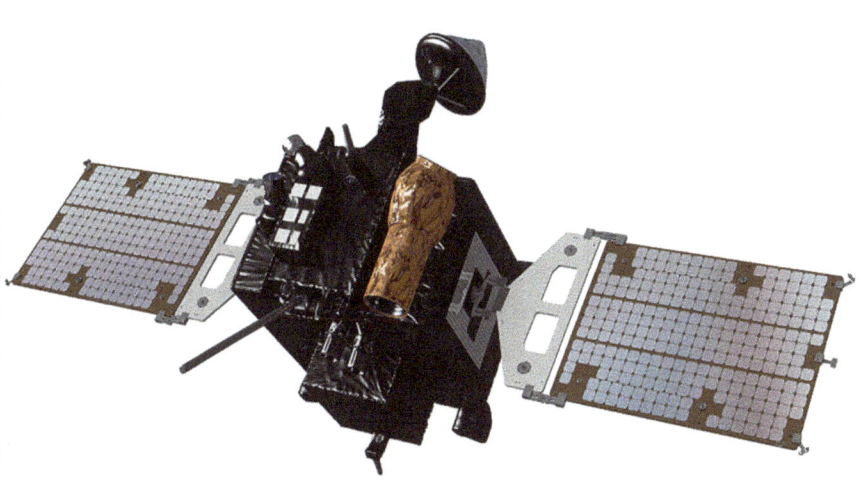

ROBOT SCIENTISTS

Today, exploration of the solar system using crewed spacecraft remains limited. But there is a fleet of unpiloted robotic devices doing the work for us. These probes explore space autonomously.

Space probes have a payload of scientific instruments and tools to collect data. These range from sensitive cameras to sensors capable of detecting specific chemicals. Probes may be designed to do their job while flying by objects in space or by orbiting and entering the atmosphere of a moon or planet. Space probes are resilient to survive extreme environments different from those on Earth. Some space probes are on a one-way trip, but others collect samples and return them to Earth. Probes have been active since the 1970's. But the newest generation of probes are discovering more about the solar system in greater detail than ever before.

Some areas of the moon, such as deep craters and its south pole, never receive any sunlight, so conventional cameras cannot capture much detail of what is there. South Korea's Danuri **orbiter** is using its high-resolution camera to see into these perpetually dark places. The goal is to identify landing sites for Korea's first crewed moon mission in the future.

PLANETARY PROBES

Saturn is surrounded by icy rings. The surface temperature on Venus is hot enough to melt lead. Many space probes have been built specifically to learn more about Earth's neighbors in space.

Mercury tag team. Mercury is the closest planet to the sun, and that makes it a difficult planet to visit. Mercury's surface temperature ranges from extreme heat to incredible cold. Probes need to travel incredibly fast to overcome the sun's powerful gravitational pull in close flybys. The BepiColombo mission launched in 2018 will approach Mercury using two orbiters. One orbiter has sensors to study the planet's form. For example, a laser altimeter will measure landforms and map the surface. The second probe will study Mercury's magnetic field and how it interacts with the solar wind. The two orbiters will autonomously combine and compare data to achieve a more complete study than any single probe.

The Hope probe of the Emirates Mars Mission entered orbit around Mars in 2021. The probe is around the size of a small car, with large solar arrays. The mission is part of long-term plans to colonize Mars one day. Its sensors study daily and seasonal weather cycles and Martian climate change. For example, hydrogen and oxygen escape from Mars's atmosphere into space. Understanding this loss of gas will help us understand why there is no liquid water on Mars today, but there is ice. Any plan to visit Mars will depend on a supply of Martian water.

Shaking the JUICE. The Jupiter Icy Moons Explorer (JUICE) orbiter's mission is to study three icy moons around Jupiter. JUICE is the size of two tennis courts including its giant solar arrays. Jupiter is the largest planet in our solar system with a gravitational force that pulls 92 moons into its orbit. Three of these are coated with thick ice beneath which there may be salty oceans. JUICE was taken to space folded up inside its launch vehicle in 2023. But once in space, it could not unfold a key part of its payload—a 52-foot- (16-meter-) wide radar antenna for scanning underneath ice. So mission control commanded the orbiter to fire its engine a few times. This shook loose a pin that kept the radar from unfolding—a successful start to JUICE's 10-year mission!

Long-distance survivor. In 1977, a probe named Voyager 1 was launched with a mission to explore Jupiter and Saturn. It continued flying since then. Today, it is the most distant human-made object—at over 14 billion miles (22.5 billion kilometers) away. Some of its equipment was switched off to save power. But it is still sending back data about interstellar space beyond our solar system!

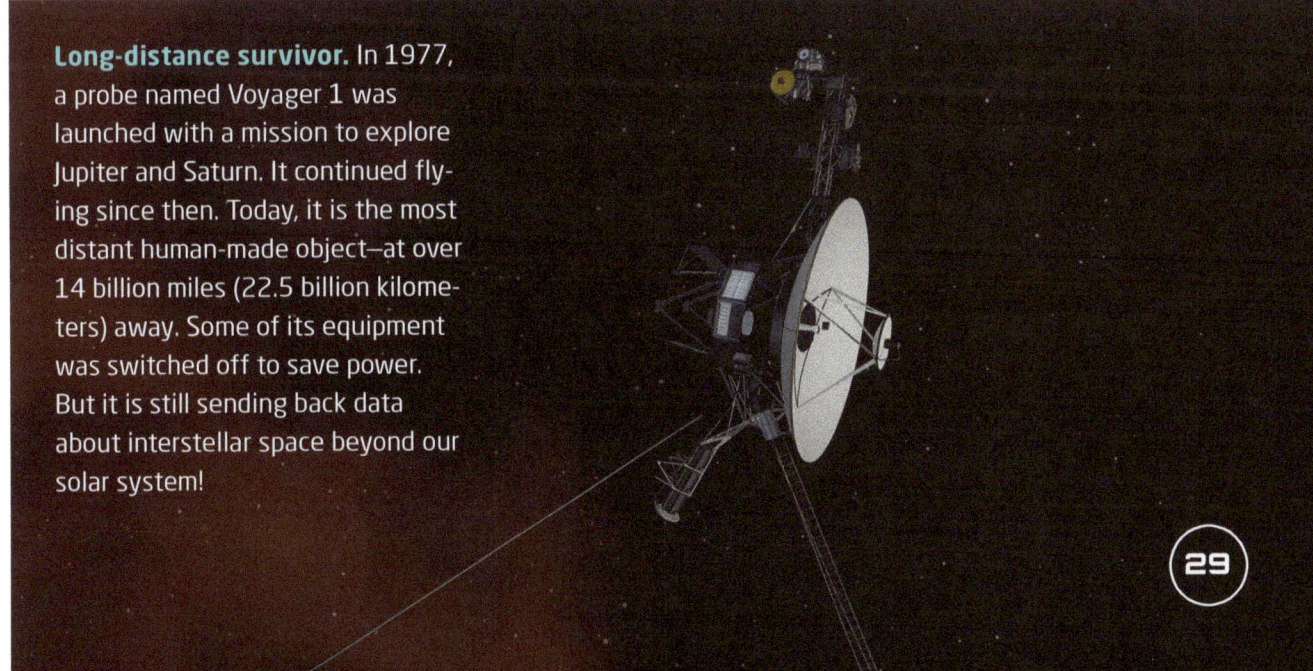

ASTEROID PROBE

Asteroids are ancient leftovers from the era of planet formation. They may contain such chemicals as carbon that are necessary ingredients for life. Scientists can study asteroid fragments that hit Earth as meteorites. But the phenomenally high-speed impact can alter the chemical composition of the rock. Space technology is coming to the rescue by taking samples directly from asteroids!

Touch-and-go. NASA launched the probe OSIRIS-REx to the asteroid Bennu. The probe's name stands for Origins Spectral Interpretation Resource Identification Security Regolith Explorer. OSIRIS-REx has sensors to map the chemistry and form of Bennu. But its most important payload is its TAGSAM arm. This is a touch-and-go sampling arm. TAGSAM is designed to penetrate the asteroid's surface to suck up material. TAGSAM blows nitrogen gas to stir up the dust on the surface and vacuum it up. OSIRIS-REx reached Bennu in late 2018 and will return a sample of it to Earth in 2023.

Catching a speeding asteroid is an incredibly complex mission. OSIRIS-REx launched in 2016 and executed several complicated course changes using its thrusters to adjust its trajectory to match that of the target asteroid Bennu. OSIRIS-REx took two years to locate a safe landing site among the boulders littering the asteroid's surface. The mission was planned so that the probe would meet up with Bennu when it was closest to Earth. The timing was crucial—one wrong maneuver, and the probe would miss its rendezvous and shoot off into space.

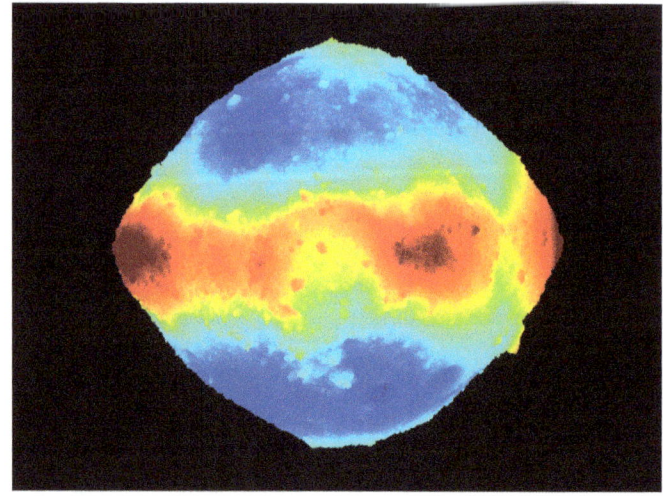

Home delivery. In 2020, OSIRIS-REx inched closer to Bennu. TAGSAM unfolded and made contact for a few seconds, but sensors found that the surface was composed of loose rubble instead of hard rock. OSIRIS-REx had to fire thrusters to prevent sinking into the asteroid. TAGSAM then successfully collected dust and pebbles from Bennu's surface. OSIRIS-REx packed the sample safely in the sample return capsule (SRC) and headed home. The SRC is due to return to Earth in late 2023. OSIRIS-REx will go on to sample another asteroid named Apophis in 2029.

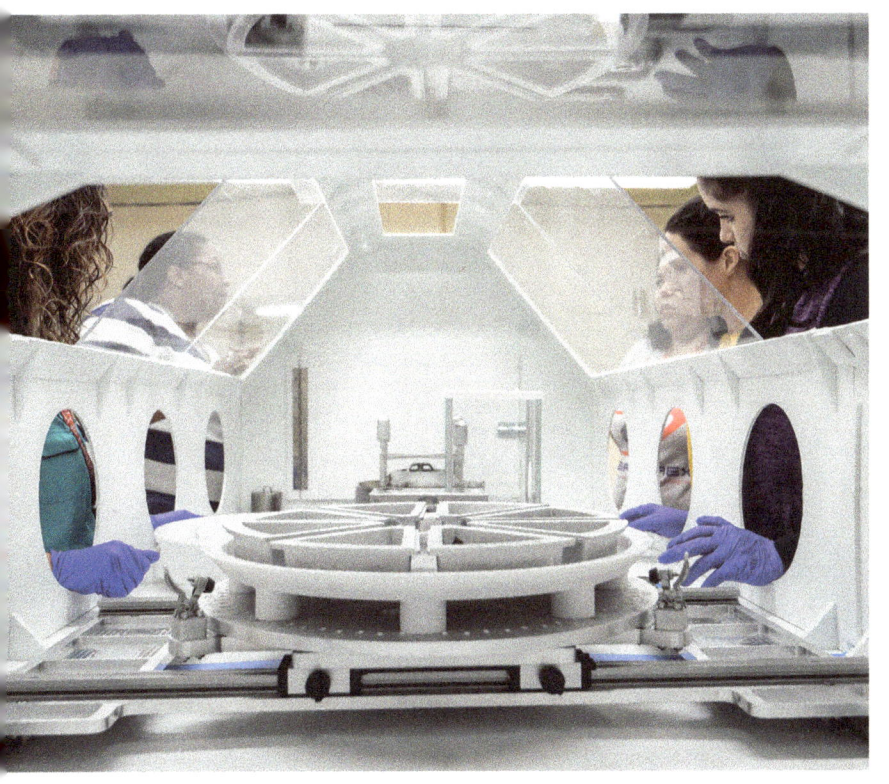

Favor for a favor. The demand for a Bennu sample is great among scientists and collectors around the world. Some space agencies contributed to the OSIRIS-REx mission in return for a few grams of asteroid material. For example, Canada provided a laser altimeter for OSIRIS-REx to produce three-dimensional (3D) maps of Bennu. Once the SRC is recovered, American technicians will transport it to Johnson Space Center in Houston. The capsule will be opened, and the sample will be cataloged and stored. This will happen in a specially built laboratory with conditions that preserve the sample chemistry. Some of the sample will be distributed. But most will be retained at Johnson for future generations to study.

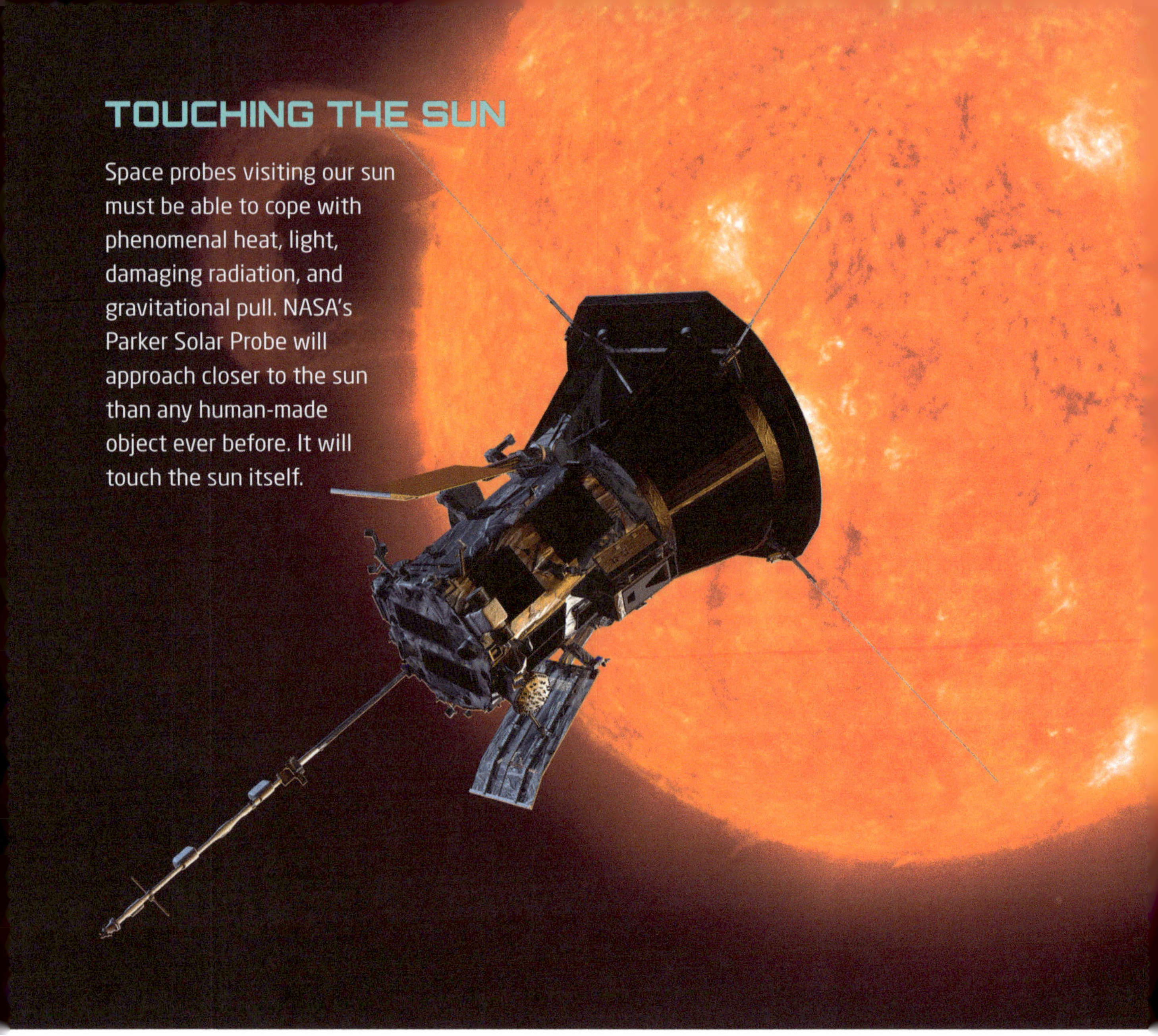

TOUCHING THE SUN

Space probes visiting our sun must be able to cope with phenomenal heat, light, damaging radiation, and gravitational pull. NASA's Parker Solar Probe will approach closer to the sun than any human-made object ever before. It will touch the sun itself.

Parker's journey. The Parker Solar Probe is around half the weight of an automobile. It was launched into space in 2018 and embarked on a wide orbit to circle the sun. This was the start of a seven-year journey to get as close to the sun as possible. The Parker Solar Probe uses the gravitational pull of Venus to gradually shrink its orbit around the sun. At its closest point in 2025, the probe will orbit within 3.8 million miles of the sun. Parker will orbit the sun 24 times. Its instruments record data during each orbit.

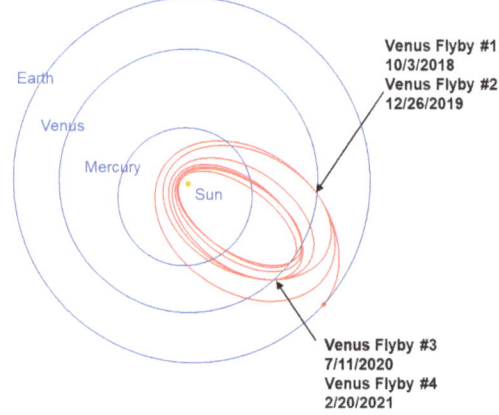

Earth
Venus
Mercury
Sun
Venus Flyby #1
10/3/2018
Venus Flyby #2
12/26/2019
Venus Flyby #3
7/11/2020
Venus Flyby #4
2/20/2021

Built to survive. Temperatures at the edge of the sun reach nearly 2500 °F (1377 °C). Parker is equipped with a 4.5-inch (11-centimeter) carbon-composite heat shield. This protects the probe's systems from damaging heat. Underneath the shield, it remains at room temperature. Parker is exposed to light 475 times brighter than the light we receive on Earth. The shield blocks the intense light from hitting and blinding the delicate instruments. Parker's solar arrays fold and unfold to generate power for the onboard systems without exposing them to too much heat.

Mission payload. The primary science goal for the Parker mission is to increase our understanding of the sun's **corona** and the origin and evolution of the solar wind—the flow of electrically charged particles from the sun. The solar wind influences Earth's climate and interferes with the electrical grid on Earth and space technology.

FIELDS is an instrument with five antennae made of heat-resistant niobium alloy sticking out beyond the spacecraft's heat shield. These measure the scale and the shape of electric fields around the sun. FIELDS also has magnetometers to capture data about the sun's magnetic fields. The fluctuating field affects how the solar wind moves.

WISPR is an imaging instrument around the size of a shoebox. It takes images of plumes of hot material exploding from the sun's corona called *coronal mass ejections*. It has special mufflers around its lens to keep light from reflecting onto other parts of the craft. Scientists use the data collected by WISPR to learn about the large-scale structure of the sun's corona and solar winds.

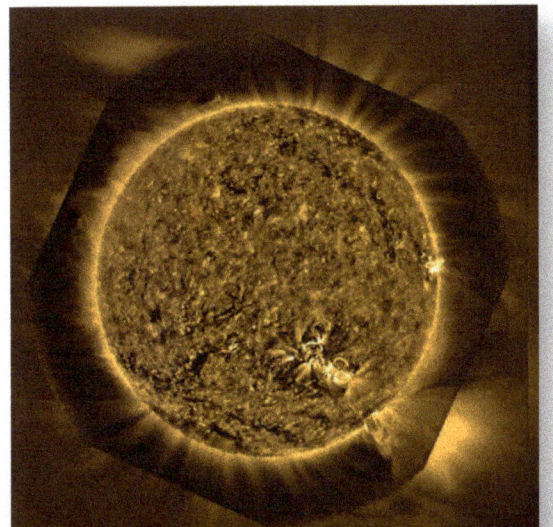

SWEAP is a Parker Solar Probe instrument used to study how energy and heat move through the sun's corona. It incorporates a solar probe cup (SPC) peeking over the heat shield. This is a vacuum cup with several high-voltage grids. These trap, sort, count, and analyze the particles that make up the solar wind. The SPC takes up to 146 measurements per second. Data from the SPC has already shown that the solar wind originates as small-scale jets shooting out from the base of the corona.

4 ROBOT LANDERS AND ROVERS

SCOUT MISSIONS

Probes rely on remote sensing technology to study conditions on a planet or other space object. But robot landers and rovers can go even further in space exploration. Their sensors can make direct measurements of an object in space. They get the closest view.

Landers are space probes that touch down on the surface of an object in space. These must be resilient to land on a moon, planet, or other space object without crashing. Some have a payload of sensors and robotic arms. Rovers are vehicles that can move around to explore the surface of an object in space. Humans have already sent dozens of landers and rovers to the moon, planets in the solar system, and even asteroids and comets. New high-tech landers and rovers promise exciting discoveries in the future.

The U.S. company Intuitive Machines specializes in lunar access and exploration. In 2023, its lander, the NOVA-C, is due to touch down on the moon. The lander is a tall, hexagonal craft with six landing legs. Its target is the edge of a crater at the moon's unexplored South Pole. The payload includes a lidar system to precisely control descent, landing, and navigation. NOVA-C's mission is to test various materials and equipment for use on the lunar surface. A receiver will test how well communication equipment will work on the moon. The data will be used to plan future crewed lunar missions. A camera onboard will capture images of the Milky Way from the moon's surface. Another remote-controlled camera on an orbiting satellite called EagleCam will take selfies of NOVA-C as it lands!

LANDERS

Sophisticated technology is necessary for robot landers to safely touch down and carry out their missions. A lander must get to its destination and decelerate to descend onto a faraway surface without damaging the payload of sensitive instruments. Once it has arrived safely, a lander must be operated by remote control to perform its mission.

Descent challenges. Not all landings are successful. Many space agencies have had lander missions that ended in a crash. In 2023, the first private moon landing failed. ispace's M1 lander fired its main engine to decelerate its orbit around the moon. A programmed sequence of commands adjusted the lander's position above the lunar surface and decelerated it further using smaller retro thrusters. But onboard instruments miscalculated the lander's altitude as it descended to the moon. M1 unexpectedly accelerated when the retro thrusters ran out of fuel, and it crashed on the lunar surface.

Mars landers need to survive the heat generated by the descent into the planet's atmosphere. Landers typically have a circular aeroshell—a heat-shielded shell. But a slower descent generates less heat that can damage the lander. NASA has experimented with an inflatable low-density supersonic decelerator. This is an inflatable doughnut around the lander that increases its surface area to slow it down. The doughnut is heat-shielded to protect the payload and deploys parachutes to slow the lander's descent. Once deployed, the lander descends to a gentle landing on the planet's surface.

Mars underground. NASA's Mars InSight lander operated from 2018 to 2022. InSight stands for Interior Exploration Using Seismic Investigations, Geodesy, and Heat Transport. The lander's instruments recorded data on the crust and interior to help answer questions about how Mars formed. InSight's payload included radio sensors to detect any wobble as Mars rotated on its axis. The size and direction of the wobble allowed scientists on Earth to calculate the size and composition of the planet's core.

Marsquake. The other key InSight instrument was the Seismic Experiment for Interior Structure (SEIS). SEIS is a dome-shaped instrument to record the seismic vibrations of Mars known as *marsquakes*. SEIS was calibrated with sensors onboard InSight. These measured wind, pressure, temperature, and magnetic field. The sensors helped SEIS distinguish between marsquakes and other phenomena that could cause vibrations, such as wind-driven dust devils on Mars. SEIS recorded hundreds of marsquakes over several years. Among these was the a magnitude 5 quake on May 5, 2022. This was the biggest ever detected on a planet other than Earth!

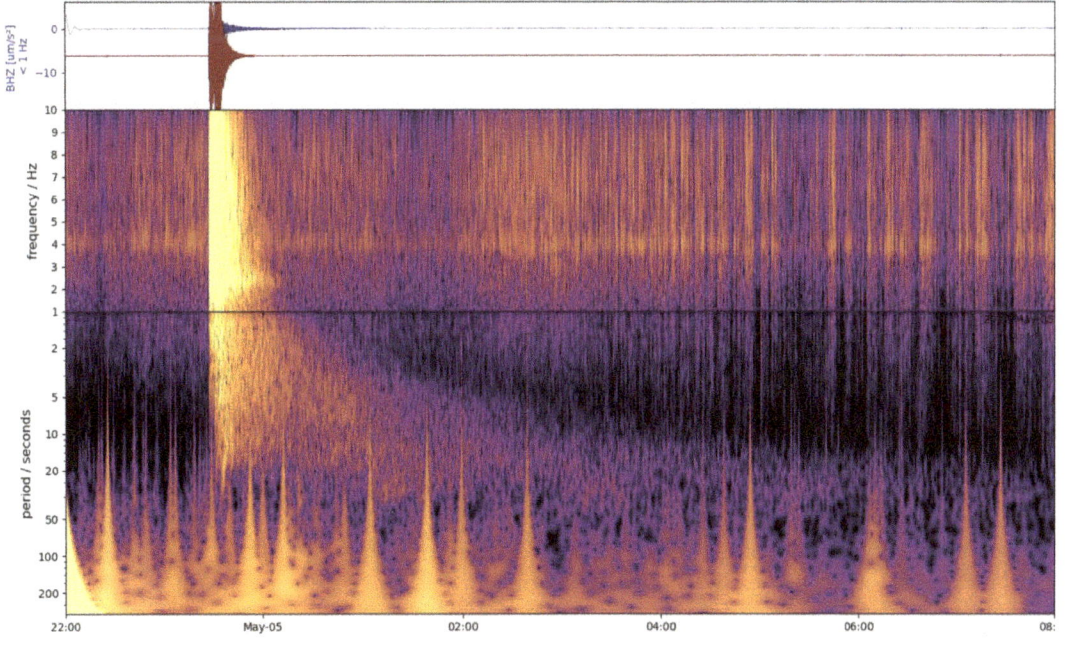

ROVERS

The moon and Mars are crisscrossed with the tracks left by rovers (vehicles). Most rovers are active for a short time and then run out of power. But some keep going well beyond the original mission. NASA's Mars Curiosity rover was deployed on the planet's surface in 2012. As of 2020, the rover had traveled more than 21 miles (34 kilometers) while exploring the Martian surface. And it is still going! There are many other rovers in action on Mars today and into the future.

Moon droid. SORA-Q is a tiny moon rover that resembles the rolling droids in the *Star Wars* films. It is a globe-shaped rover the size of a baseball. SORA-Q splits open into two connected hemispheres that act as its wheels. SORA-Q has a tail that drags on the ground to keep the rover from toppling over. The rod connecting the two hemispheres incorporates a flip-up camera to take pictures of the moon and transmit them to Earth. But SORA-Q was carried on the 2023 M1 lander that crashed. So the design will have to wait for a future mission.

Modular moon rovers. Moon rovers are expensive to build. But Astrobotic builds modular rovers in standard sizes that are more affordable. Like **CubeSats** (small modular cubic satellites), the rovers are made up of cubic modular units measuring 4 inches (10 centimeters). They use standard off the shelf parts instead of custom-built parts, and they are adaptable to many different payloads. CubeRovers are as light as 8.8 pounds (4 kilograms). Astrobotic's Polaris rovers are larger to carry more payload and go farther. They have inbuilt cameras, solar panels, and antennae for basic functionality.

NASA's Perseverance rover landed gently on Mars in 2021, suspended from a platform with multiple retro thrusters. This car-sized rover rolls on six titanium wheels, each with a separate motor, springy suspension, and ridges for traction on the uneven regolith. Perseverance's mission is to look for signs that liquid water and life once existed on Mars. A tall mast on top of Perseverance has cameras to help navigate and for recording high-definition video. The largest, SuperCam, incorporates a camera, laser, and spectrometer (instrument to study light). The laser fires powerful light beams at rocks up to 21 feet (7 meters) away. The intense light vaporizes the rock into particles that emit light. Different chemicals in the rocks produce different light patterns that the spectrometer can distinguish. Perseverance has two identical computer units, so it can always operate its sophisticated payload and autonomously explore even if one stops working.

Ingenuity. A buddy rover named Ingenuity was stowed onboard Perseverance. Ingenuity is a *drone* (unpiloted aerial vehicle). It is the first rotorcraft robot to fly somewhere other than Earth. It has two 4-foot- (1.2-meter-) long counterrotating blades that provide lift against the thin Martian atmosphere. Ingenuity was designed primarily to prove a Mars flight would work. But the drone has gone on to scout for other locations for Perseverance to drive to.

CHINA'S MARS MISSION

The Chinese National Space Administration's Tianwen-1 mission launched in 2020. Its orbiter and rover reached Mars in May 2021—within days of NASA's Perseverance. This was no coincidence. Every 26 months, Earth and Mars are aligned on the same side of the sun and closer together in their orbits. Any missions launched from Earth have a shorter, more fuel-efficient path to Mars. Even so, this was the first time in history that any two nations sent both a lander and rover to a planet at the same time!

Zhurong. China's Tianwen-1 orbiter used high-resolution cameras to find a suitable rover landing site on Mars. The site had to be a flat area with good visibility and low wind—and interesting surroundings. The orbiter released the lander to touch down on the Utopia Planitia plain. Scientists think this area was once an ocean on Mars. The lander extended ramps, and the rover—named Zhurong—drove off. A Mars climate station on top of the rover monitored temperature, wind speed, and direction, and air pressure on a MarA microphone recorded the wind blowing and other sounds on Mars.

Power down. Zhurong has large fold-out solar panels something like an insect's wings for generating power. But in May 2022, it folded up the wings and powered down. The reason is the chilly weather and intense dust storms of the Martian winter. Zhurong can go into a low-power hibernation mode to save energy. The rover should power up again once the temperature rises. Unfortunately, dust buildup on the solar panels prevented them from receiving enough light to power up. Zhurong does have equipment to shake the wings to make dust fall off. But these didn't work because it was powered down! As of May 2023, Zhurong has not been able to function.

Instruments. Zhurong used a variety of high-tech instruments to explore Mars as it drove southward from its landing site up to 30 feet (10 meters) per day. Zhurong's ground-penetrating radar directed radio waves under the surface and measured the reflection. The data allows scientists on Earth to piece together a 3D map of what lies beneath. The rover contained a material called n-undecane, which stored heat from the solar panels and released it at night. This kept the sensitive instruments warm, so that they could function properly during the frigid Martian night.

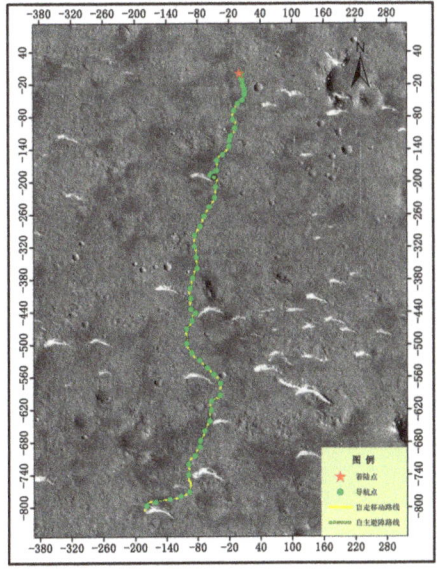

An ancient ocean may once have stretched over Utopia Planitia. Scientists analyzing the data from Zhurong's instruments discovered hydrated minerals in a hard layer on the Martian surface. This duricrust forms after groundwater evaporates. Scientists also observed ridges and cracks on the crust created by thawing frost or snow. Other observed properties of the Martian regolith suggest erosion by water. The data collected by Zhurong suggests that liquid water existed on Mars as recently as 400,000 years ago.

5 SPACE OBSERVATORIES

BETTER VIEWPOINT

One of the fundamental questions for humans is: Are we alone in the universe? A major aim of space exploration is to discover new planets and unmistakable signs of extraterrestrial life. Probes, landers, and crewed spacecraft today cannot study planets beyond our solar system—called exoplanets. We rely on new high-tech observatories to see these and the outer reaches of the universe. New observatories are under construction. Some are built on Earth, and others will be launched into space.

The Giant Magellan Telescope (GMT) in Chile is an Earth-based observatory that should be operational by 2029. It will use seven of the world's largest mirrors and will be 200 times more powerful than the best ground-based telescopes today. And it will have a special adaptive optics system to correct for the blurring effect of Earth's atmosphere. LuSEE-Night is a prototype radio telescope that will operate from a lander on the dark side of the moon. Here it can receive faint radio signals from the universe without interference. Some of these signals will be from the Cosmic Dark Ages. This is a time just after the big bang when the universe was still forming—before bright stars and galaxies appeared. LuSEE-Night could help us better understand how the universe evolved.

SPACE TELESCOPES

The GMT in Chile will push the limits of Earth-based telescope technology. It rivals the resolution power of the biggest telescopes on Earth and even that of the Hubble and the James Webb Space telescopes. These telescopes operate in space, beyond the blurring effects of Earth's atmosphere, to provide images of our universe with stunning clarity. But their capabilities will be dwarfed by the new generation of space telescopes.

Shape-shifter. In general, the bigger the mirror, the greater the resolution of a telescope. The size of the James Webb Space Telescope (JWST) was limited because it had to be carried into space on a rocket. But scientists ingeniously designed the JWST's huge mirror to fold up so it could fit on a rocket. Once in space, the mirror unfolded, and actuators on the back adjusted its shape to focus correctly. Scientists are now designing space telescope mirrors that can be constructed from separate components launched into space. These future mirrors will be made of smart materials that shape-shift as electric current flows through them, without actuators.

Next scope. NASA's Nancy Grace Roman Space Telescope (RST) is scheduled for launch in 2027. It has a similar-sized mirror compared to the Hubble Space Telescope but outperforms it remarkably. RST's Wide Field Instrument will be able to image an area of sky 100 times larger than Hubble. So a single RST image will be 100 times more detailed. RST will measure light from a billion galaxies and seek thousands of exoplanets in the Milky Way. RST's Coronograph is a specialized instrument that measures the light from exoplanets near bright stars. These exoplanets are 100 billion times fainter than the distant stars they orbit.

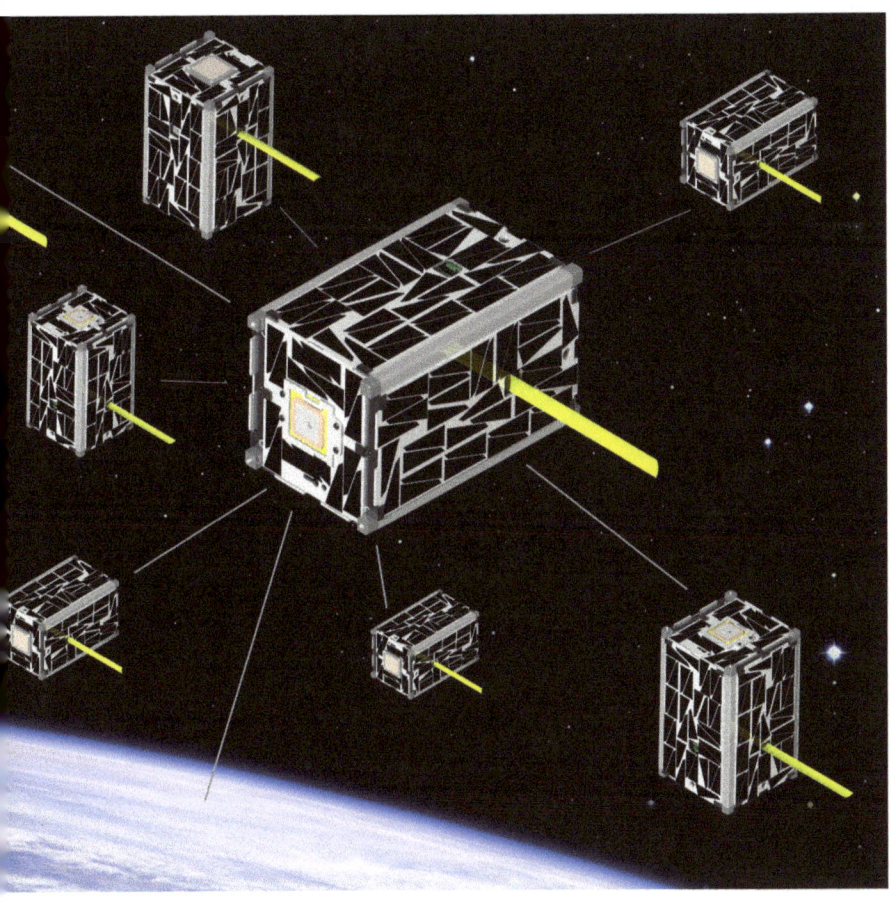

Swarm scope. Rather than design a bigger and better space telescope, some scientists propose another approach—using a swarm of CubeSats to form a space telescope. HaloSat is a CubeSat designed to detect X-ray emissions from objects in deep space. Between 2018 and 2021, it surveyed the entire sky and mapped the X-ray halos produced by structures in distant galaxies. Scientists think that a swarm of such CubeSats can orbit Earth in formation connected by inter-satellite links. Working together, they can detect distant objects in the universe and generate data to create an image to send to Earth. Soon, swarms of HaloSats or other CubeSats may function as giant space telescopes to produce images of distant objects with amazing clarity.

Solar gravity lenses. The most advanced new space telescopes will use the gravitational might of our sun to focus light from objects incredibly far away. This is the theory behind a space telescope equipped with a solar gravity lens. Such a telescope will not use traditional mirrors, lenses, or optics to focus light. Instead, it will use the gravity of the sun. Astronomers have long known that the gravitational pull of massive objects in space bends the light coming from a more distant object. Scientists envision a telescope in deep space that could align itself with the sun and a distant object. The sun's gravity acts like a lens to focus light waves from the object so it can be imaged. Such a solar gravity lens could produce images 1,000 times clearer than the most modern telescopes used currently.

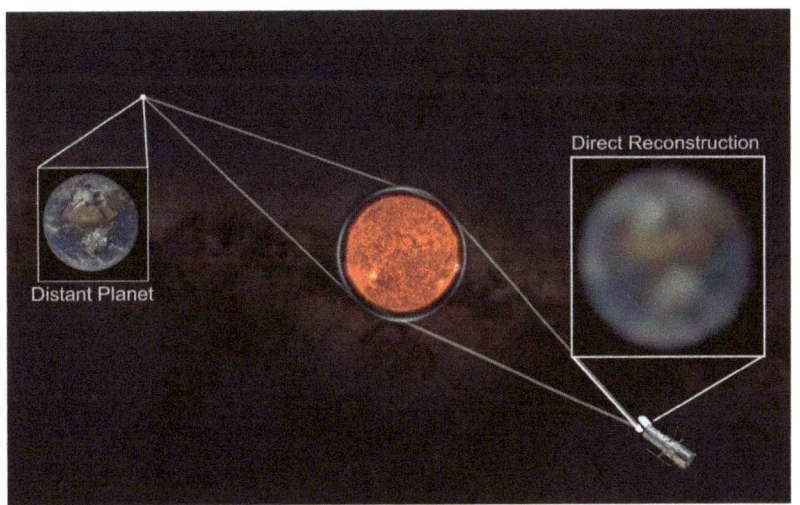

ENGAGE YOUR READER

Nonfiction writing often includes subject-specific vocabulary terms. Knowing the words related to the topic helps us understand the text itself.

When good readers come upon words they don't know well, they pause and try to figure them out. One tool they use is the glossary, like the one on page 4. Not every word can be defined in a glossary, though!

Authors know this, so they leave clues about words in the text. Next time you encounter a challenging word, stop and look for information about its meaning in the surrounding sentences. Sometimes authors define the term right there in the text! Other times, they'll compare the term to something you may already know. Authors even use punctuation like commas or dashes to clue you in to a word's meaning.

INSTRUCTIONS

1. Consider the list of challenge words and identify where each is used in the text. You can use the Index on page 48 to help you locate each term.

2. Explain how the author described each word. Ask yourself "what is happening in the text?" or "how is this word being used?" as you search for clues about their meanings.

3. Create your own definitions of the words. Don't just copy the dictionary definitions. Instead think about how you would tell a friend what each term means.

4. Add a visual representation for each word. Think about what you could draw that will help you remember what the words mean.

Visit www.worldbook.com/resources to download your own graphic organizer as well as other free resources!

CHALLENGE WORDS

- Atmosphere
- Payload
- Module
- Propulsion
- Thrust
- Navigation
- Mission
- Low Earth orbit (LEO)

EXAMPLE

Challenge Word	Page(s)	Author's Description	Personal Definition	Visual Representation
Atmosphere	7-8, 15-16, 20, 27-28, 36, 39, 43-44	- outer layers of gas around Earth and other planets - gas or air surrounding a planet	The layers of gas that are found above Earth.	
Payload				

INDEX

A
airlocks, 13, 19
antennae, 17, 23, 29, 38
Artemis, 14, 22, 24
asteroids, 30, 31
astronauts, 7, 9, 10-13, 15, 16, 19, 20, 22, 24
atmosphere, 7, 8, 15, 16, 20, 27, 28, 36, 39, 43, 44
autonomous, 16, 21, 22, 27, 28, 39

B
Bennu, 30-31
blast shields, 20, 22

C
capsules, 20-23, 31
cargo, 7, 10, 12, 20
Chinese, 8, 9, 16, 20, 40
Chinese Space Station (CSS), 9, 20
CubeSats, 38, 45
Curiosity, 38

D
deep space, 19, 21-23, 45
docking, 8, 10, 12, 15
dust, 25, 30, 31, 37, 41

G
Gateway (moon space station), 14, 15
GPS (satellites), 10, 23

H
habitation, 10, 13, 15, 19
heat shields, 33, 36

I
ice, 28, 29
inflatable, 12, 36
Ingenuity, 39

International Space Station (ISS), 7, 8, 16, 20

J
James Webb Space Telescope (JWST), 44
Jupiter, 29

L
landers (space), 34-38, 40, 43
laser, 28, 31, 39

M
magnetic field, 28, 37
Mars, 14, 19, 21, 28, 36-41
Mercury, 28
microgravity, 7, 10
missions, 8-10, 14-17, 19, 21, 22, 24, 27-31, 33, 35, 36, 38-40
modular, 11, 38
modules, 7, 9, 15, 17, 22, 23
moon, 14, 15, 19, 20, 22, 24, 25, 27, 29, 35, 36, 38, 43

N
navigation, 23, 35, 39

O
orbiters (space), 27, 28, 29, 40
Orion, 22-23, 24
OSIRIS-REx, 30-31
Outpost (moon base camp), 14, 15, 17
oxygen, 7, 25, 28

P
parachutes, 20, 21, 36
Parker Solar Probe, 32-33
payload, 10, 15, 27, 29, 30, 33, 35-39
Perseverance, 39

probes (space), 28-30, 32, 33
propulsion, 12, 15, 21, 23

R
radiation, 8, 21, 24, 25, 32
regolith, 25, 30, 39, 41
robotic arms, 12, 15, 16, 17, 35
rockets, 10, 16, 17, 20, 21, 23, 44
rovers (space), 34, 35, 38, 39, 40, 41

S
satellites, 10, 13, 16, 17, 38
sensors, 27, 28, 30, 31, 35, 37
solar arrays, 9, 15, 23, 28, 33
solar cells, 9, 25
space agencies, 12, 16, 31, 36
space junk, 16, 17
space telescopes, 44, 45
SpaceX Dragon, 20
stages (rocket), 16, 17
Starlab, 12-13
sun, 32-33, 45

T
taikonauts, 9, 20
thrusters, 15, 20, 23, 30, 31, 36, 39
Tiangong Space Station (TSS), 7
Tianwen-1, 40-41
trajectories, 23, 30

V
Venus, 28, 32
Voyager 1, 29

W
water, 7, 15, 28, 39, 41

Z
Zhurong, 40-41

www.ingramcontent.com/pod-product-compliance
Lightning Source LLC
Chambersburg PA
CBHW041139170426
43198CB00023B/2986